DATE DUE

AUG 2 5 2010		
AUG 2 0 2016		
OCT 1 5 2016		
MAR 2 5 2017		

Demco, Inc. 38-293

SLIM GOODBODY'S NUTRITION EDITION

Outstanding Oils and Wonderful Water

CRABTREE
Publishing Company
www.crabtreebooks.com

![Crabtree Publishing Company logo]

Crabtree Publishing Company
www.crabtreebooks.com

Series development, writing, and packaging:
John Burstein, Slim Goodbody Corp.

Editors:
Molly Aloian
Reagan Miller
Mark Sachner, Water Buffalo Books

Editorial director:
Kathy Middleton

Production coordinator:
Kenneth Wright

Prepress technician:
Kenneth Wright

Designer:
Tammy West, Westgraphix LLC

Photos:
Chris Pinchback, Pinchback Photography

Photo credits:
© Slim Goodbody, iStockphotos, and Shutterstock images.

"Slim Goodbody" and Pinchback photos, copyright,
© Slim Goodbody

Acknowledgements:
The author would like to thank the following people for
their help in this project:
Christine Burstein, Olivia Davis, Kylie Fong, Nathan
Levig, Havana Lyman, Andrew McBride, Lulu McClure,
Ben McGinnis, Esme Power, Joe Ryan

"Slim Goodbody" and "Slim Goodbody's Nutrition Edition"
are registered trademarks of the Slim Goodbody Corp.

Library and Archives Canada Cataloguing in Publication

Burstein, John
    Outstanding oils and wonderful water / John Burstein.

(Slim Goodbody's nutrition edition) Includes index.
ISBN 978-0-7787-5046-8 (bound).--ISBN 978-0-7787-5061-1 (pbk.)

    1. Vegetable oils in human nutrition--Juvenile literature. 2. Lipids in
human nutrition--Juvenile literature. 3. Nutrition--Juvenile literature.
4. Water--Physiological effect--Juvenile literature. I. Title. II. Series:°Burstein,
John. Slim Goodbody's nutrition edition.

QP144.O44B87 2010   j613.2'84   C2009-903857-9

Library of Congress Cataloging-in-Publication Data

Burstein, John.
    Outstanding oils and wonderful water / John Burstein.
       p. cm. -- (Slim Goodbody's nutrition edition)
    Includes index.
    ISBN 978-0-7787-5046-8 (reinforced lib. bdg. : alk. paper) -- ISBN 978-0-
7787-5061-1 (pbk. : alk. paper)
    1. Vegetable oils in human nutrition--Juvenile literature. 2. Lipids in human
nutrition--Juvenile literature. 3. Nutrition--Juvenile literature. 4. Water--
Physiological effect--Juvenile literature. 5. Children--Nutrition--Require-
ments--Juvenile literature. I. Title. II. Series.

QP144.O44B87 2010
613.2'84--dc22
                                        2009024572

Crabtree Publishing Company
www.crabtreebooks.com   1-800-387-7650

Published in Canada
Crabtree Publishing
616 Welland Ave.
St. Catharines, Ontario
L2M 5V6

Published in the United States
Crabtree Publishing
PMB16A
350 Fifth Ave., Suite 3308
New York, NY 10118

Published in the United Kingdom
Crabtree Publishing
White Cross Mills
High Town, Lancaster
LA1 4XS

Published in Australia
Crabtree Publishing
386 Mt. Alexander Rd.
Ascot Vale (Melbourne)
VIC 3032

CONTENTS

GREETINGS

My name is Slim Goodbody.
I want to ask you two questions.

1. Do you want to be healthy?
I hope you said **YES**.

2. If you do not eat right, can
you be healthy?
I hope you said **NO**.

The U.S. food pyramid helps you eat right.

There are six stripes on the U.S. food pyramid.

The stripes stand for the five different food groups plus oils.

GRAINS
VEGETABLES
FRUITS
OILS
MILK
MEAT
&BEANS

This book is about oils and water.

OILS!

Oils belong on the yellow stripe in the U.S. food pyramid. Oils are not a food group. Oils are a liquid. They are found in plants and other foods.

We need some oils every day.

We can get the oils we need from different foods.

NUTS
hazelnuts
peanuts
almonds

FISH
salmon
lake trout
albacore tuna

COOKING OILS
olive oil
sunflower oil

SALAD DRESSINGS
italian dressing

AROUND THE WORLD

NORTH
AMERICA

walnuts

avocados

SOUTH
AMERICA

peanuts

Plants with oils grow all around the world.

8

olives

sesame seeds

ASIA

EUROPE

AFRICA

soybeans

almonds

cashews

hazelnuts

AUSTRALIA

The same kind of plants can come from many places.

9

OILS KEEP YOU HEALTHY

You need oils to help keep your body healthy and active.

Oils help different body parts.

Oils help protect your
heart and blood vessels.

Oils help you store
up energy to get
things done.

Oils help keep
your skin soft.

Oils help protect you
from illness.

Oils help your
brain work well.

YOU NEED OILS EACH DAY

You need four teaspoons (20 ml) of oils each day. Most people do not put foods onto teaspoons. So here is another way to figure out how to get the oils you need.

FOUR TEASPOONS EQUALS ABOUT:

28 almonds

20 hazelnuts

24 cashews

37 peanuts

32 large olives

1 1/2 tablespoons of margarine

2 tablespoons of peanut butter

1 1/3 tablespoons of vegetable oils like olive oil, sunflower oil, and soybean oil

1 tablespoon = 15ml

Almost any time is a good time to get some oils.

You can eat a breakfast cereal with nuts.

You can have a peanut butter sandwich for lunch.

You can sprinkle some nuts on yogurt for a snack.

You can have dressing on your salad at dinner.

It is easy to get the oils you need.

WONDERFUL WATER

Like oils, water is not a food. It is not on the food pyramid.

Water helps keep your body healthy.

You need water just as much as food.

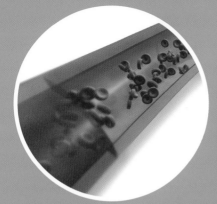

Blood is made mostly of water.

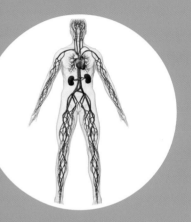

Without water, your blood would not flow.

Blood brings energy to all parts of your body.

Without water, your body would not get the energy it needs.

You need water to stay alive.

YOU NEED WATER EACH DAY

You need six to eight glasses of water a day.

Do not drink all your water at one time.

Try to drink a glass of water with each meal.

Try to drink a glass of water between each meal.

Drink water when you are thirsty.

Drink water after you exercise.

Drink water if you are sweating a lot.

You can also drink milk or 100% fruit juice.

19

EAT YOUR WATER

You do not have to get your water by drinking it. Here are some other ways to get water.

Watermelon is almost all water.

Eat vegetables.
Celery and carrots
have a lot of water.

Eat fruits. Peaches and
plums have a lot of water.

Juicy fruits have a lot of water.

WORLD FOOD GUIDES

The U.S. food pyramid is only one guide to eating well.

To learn more about Canada's Food Guide, visit the Web site below.

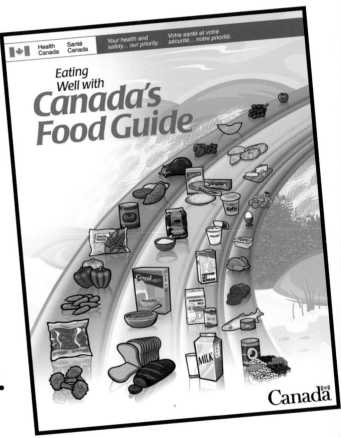

www.nms.on.ca/Elementary/canada.htm

People from different parts of the world often eat different kinds of foods. People use different food guides to help them eat wisely.

PUERTO RICAN
FOOD GUIDE PYRAMID

6-8
Glasses of water

Fats, Oils, Sweets & Sodium
Use sparingly
fried foods, chips, candy, donuts
soft drinks

Milk, Cheese & Yogurt
2-3 Servings
1 cup of milk
8 ounces of yogurt

Meat, Poultry, Fish Dry Beans, Eggs & Nuts
2-3 Servings
2-3 ounces of cooked meat, poultry, or fish
1/2 cup of cooked legumes, 1 egg

Vegetables
3-5 Servings
1/2 cup of cooked or raw veggies
1 cup of leafy raw vegetables

Fruits
2-4 Servings
1 medium size fruit
1/2 cup of berries or sliced fruits
3/4 cup of 100% fruit juice

Bread, Cereal, Pasta Rice & Viandas
6-11 Servings

1 slice of bread
1/2 cup of cooked cereal
rice or pasta
1 ounce of ready-to-eat cereal
1/2 cup of viandas

UNIVERSITY OF CONNECTICUT

Every day, everyone, everywhere needs oils and water.

WORDS TO KNOW

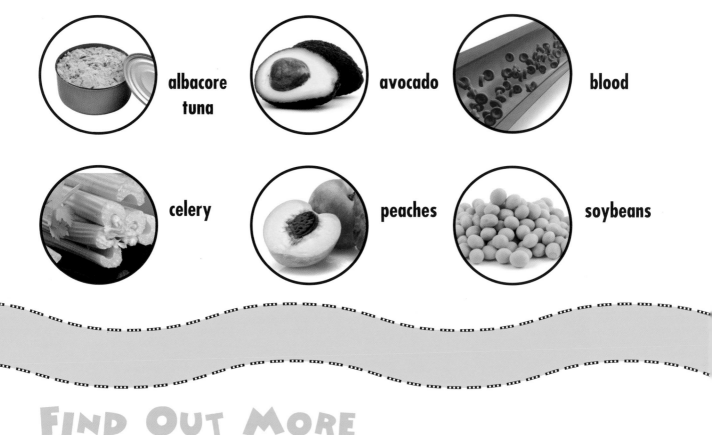

albacore tuna

avocado

blood

celery

peaches

soybeans

FIND OUT MORE

Books

Fats, Oils, And Sweets, Carol Parenzan Smalley, Children's Press.

Oils, Tea Benduhn and Susan Nations, Weekly Reader Early Learning Library.

Web Sites

MyPyramid.gov
www.mypyramid.gov/kids/index.html

Slim Goodbody
www.slimgoodbody.com

Printed in the U.S.A.-CG